NUMBER GROUPS

The horizontal lines, or rows, in this table show all the diff... combinations of two numbers that make up the numbers ... 12. They are ... ls for ... hem.

3 + 3 = 6
3 + 4 = 7   4 + 3 = 7
3 + 5 = 8   5 + 3 = 8   4 + ...
3 + 6 = 9   6 + 3 = 9   4 + 5 = 9   5 + 4 = 9
3 + 7 = 10   7 + 3 = 10   4 + 6 = 10   6 + 4 = 10   5 + 5 = 10
3 + 8 = 11   8 + 3 = 11   4 + 7 = 11   7 + 4 = 11   5 + 6 = 11   6 + 5 = 11
3 + 9 = 12   9 + 3 = 12   4 + 8 = 12   8 + 4 = 12   5 + 7 = 12   7 + 5 = 12
6 + 6 = 12

COUNTING IN 2s

2 4 6 8 10 12 14 16 18 20 22 24 26 28 30

COUNTING IN 3s

3 6 9 12 15 18 21 24 27 30 33 36 39 42 45

COUNTING IN 5s

5 10 15 20 25 30 35 40 45 50 55 60 65 70 75

COUNTING IN 7s

7 14 21 28 35 42 49 56 63 70 77 84

MESSAGE TO PARENTS

These books are designed to help children in the 6-8 age range to learn and practice their early maths skills. Basic facts about addition, subtraction, multiplication and division are presented in a clear and understandable way with the use of amusing colourful pictures, simple text and numerous games and puzzles. In this way the books can be used in the home to complement and reinforce the educational process that takes place in school.

Knowledge absorbed gradually is usually absorbed more thoroughly, so never try to cover too much in one session. It is important to make sure that your child understands each page as you progress together through the books. Always remember that learning ought to be an enjoyable experience and, in particular, maths can be and should be FUN.

First published 1995 by Brown Watson
The Old Mill
Kibworth Beauchamp
Leics LE8 0HG

ISBN: 0-7097-1082-8

Paul Annan

addition

Compiled by Colin Clark
Illustrated by Stephen Holmes

Brown Watson
ENGLAND

This is a little mouse.

This is another little mouse.

Now there are two mice.

one mouse + one mouse = two mice $\quad 1 + 1 = 2$

Here is a snail.

Along comes another snail.

Now there are two snails.

one snail + one snail = two snails $\quad 1 + 1 = 2$

REMEMBER

$1 + 1 = 2$

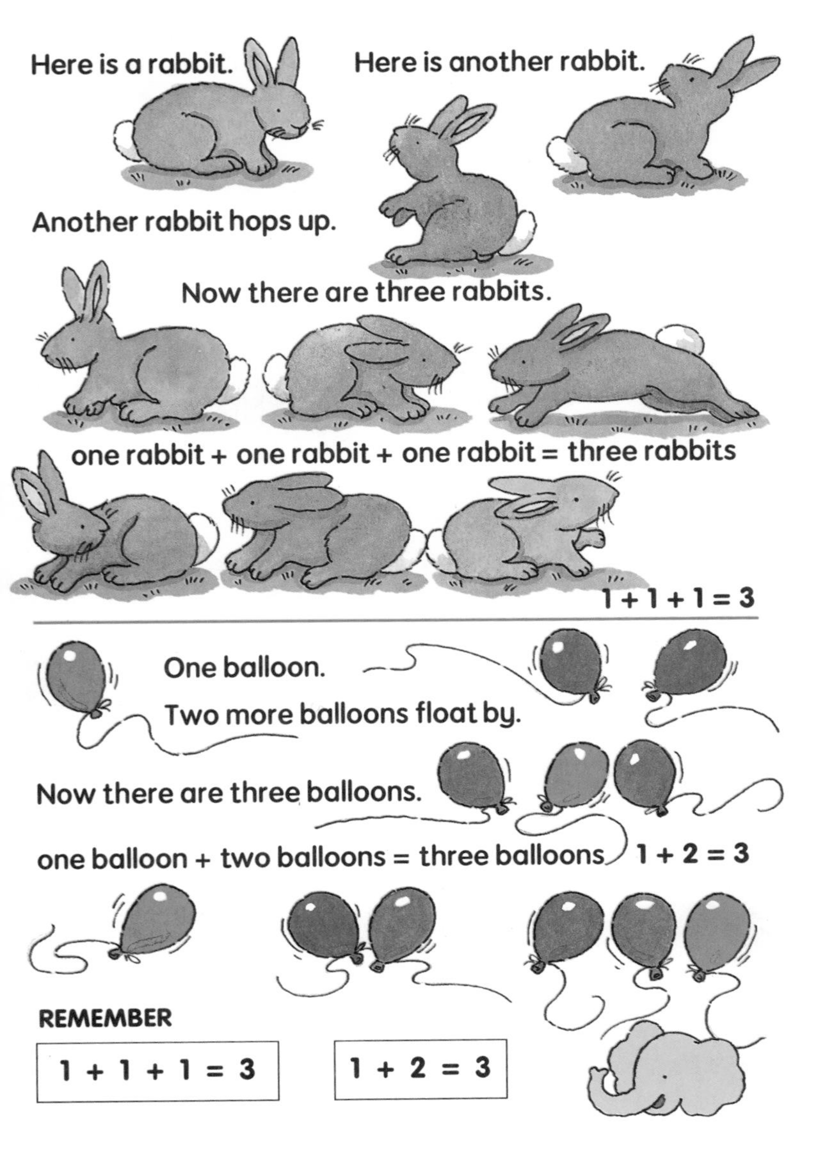
Here is a rabbit.
Here is another rabbit.
Another rabbit hops up.
Now there are three rabbits.
one rabbit + one rabbit + one rabbit = three rabbits
1 + 1 + 1 = 3
One balloon.
Two more balloons float by.
Now there are three balloons.
one balloon + two balloons = three balloons
1 + 2 = 3
REMEMBER
1 + 1 + 1 = 3
1 + 2 = 3

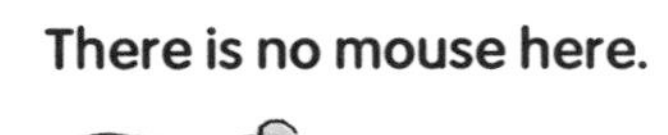

There is no mouse here.

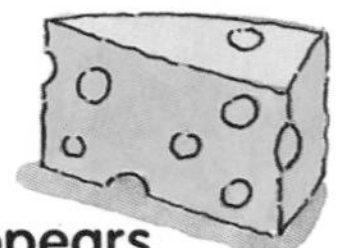

Suddenly, a mouse appears.

Now there is one mouse here.

no mouse + one mouse = one mouse $0 + 1 = 1$

There is no snail here.

Along come two snails.

Now there are two snails here.

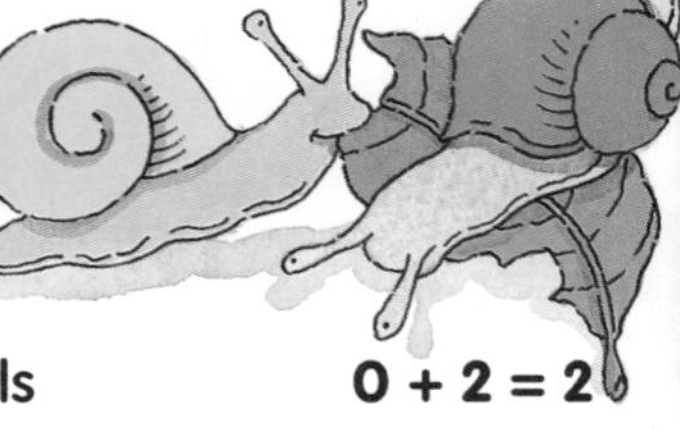

no snail + two snails = two snails $0 + 2 = 2$

REMEMBER $0 + 1 = 1$ $0 + 2 = 2$

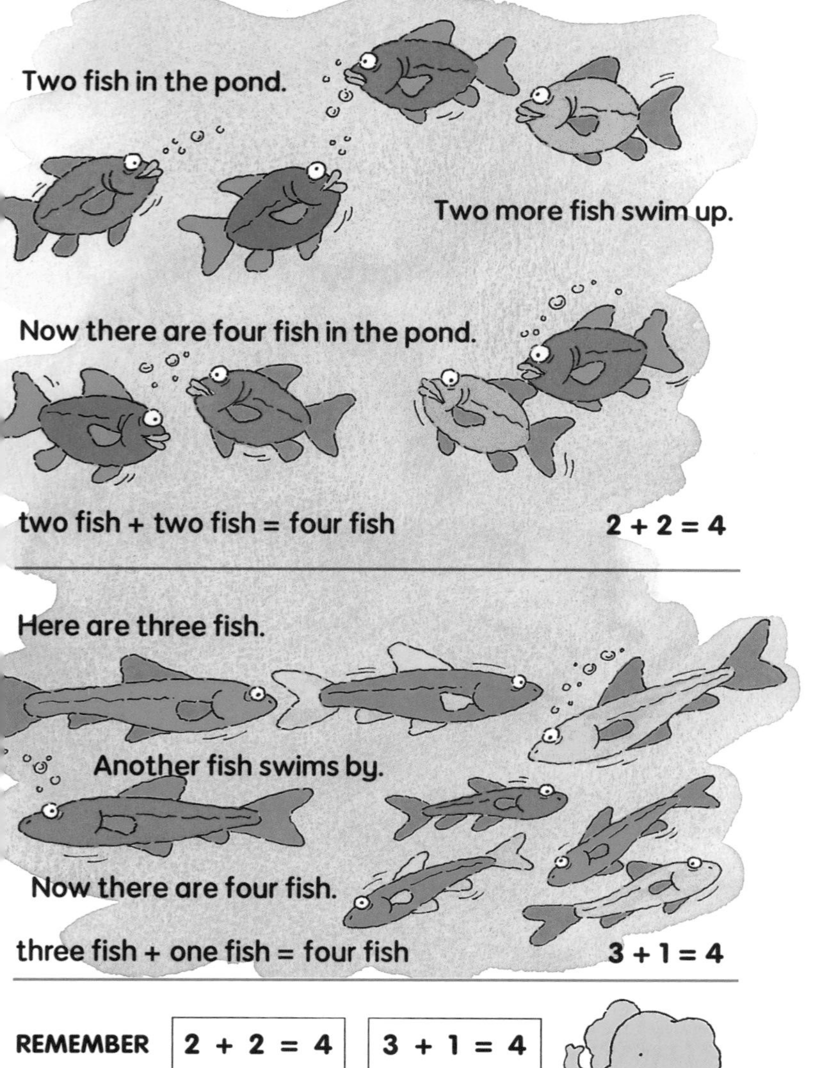

Two fish in the pond.

Two more fish swim up.

Now there are four fish in the pond.

two fish + two fish = four fish $2 + 2 = 4$

Here are three fish.

Another fish swims by.

Now there are four fish.

three fish + one fish = four fish $3 + 1 = 4$

REMEMBER $2 + 2 = 4$ $3 + 1 = 4$

There are two balls in this box.

Here are three more balls.

Now there are five balls.

two balls + three balls = five balls **2 + 3 = 5**

There are four oranges on the plate.

Here is another orange.

Now there are five oranges on the plate.

four oranges + one orange = five oranges **4 + 1 = 5**

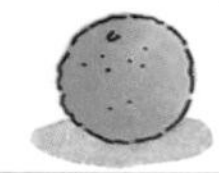

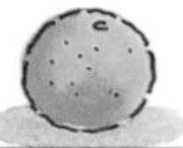

REMEMBER **2 + 3 = 5** **4 + 1 = 5**

Three little ducklings.

Another three little ducklings.

Now there are six ducklings in the water.

three ducklings + three ducklings = six ducklings

$3 + 3 = 6$

Here are four frogs.

Two more frogs hop by.

Now there are six frogs.

four frogs + two frogs = six frogs

$4 + 2 = 6$

REMEMBER $3 + 3 = 6$ $4 + 2 = 6$

Can you load the sacks onto the right lorries?

Dominoes

The spots on each of these dominoes add up to 6.
Can you fill in the missing number groups?

There are seven dominoes shown here. If all the dominoes were completed, there would be one domino for each of the numbers from **0** to **6**. Can you decide what spots are missing, if any, from the dominoes that are not completed, so that you have a full set of numbers.

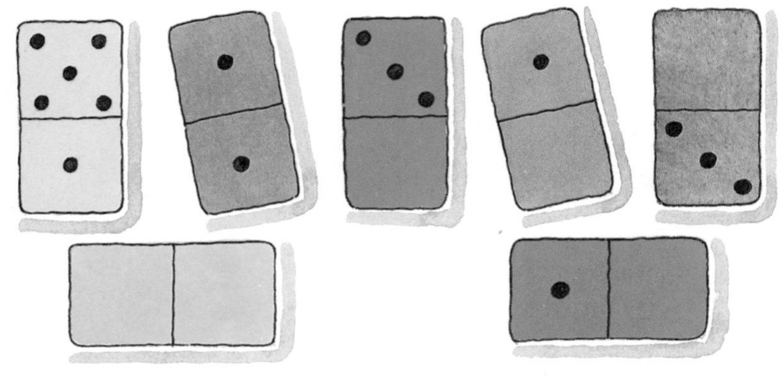

This bird's nest has four eggs in it.

There are three eggs in this nest.

There are seven eggs altogether.

four eggs + three eggs = seven eggs

$4 + 3 = 7$

This black kitten is playing with five balls of wool.

This tabby kitten has two balls of wool.

Together, the kittens have seven balls of wool.

five balls of wool + two balls of wool = seven balls of wool

$5 + 2 = 7$

REMEMBER $4 + 3 = 7$ $5 + 2 = 7$

How many dwarfs can you see in this picture?

How many dwarfs are in the woods?

If all the dwarfs are at home, how many dwarfs will be in the cottage?

Try to learn all the number bonds that make up seven. They are marked on the points of the snowflake.

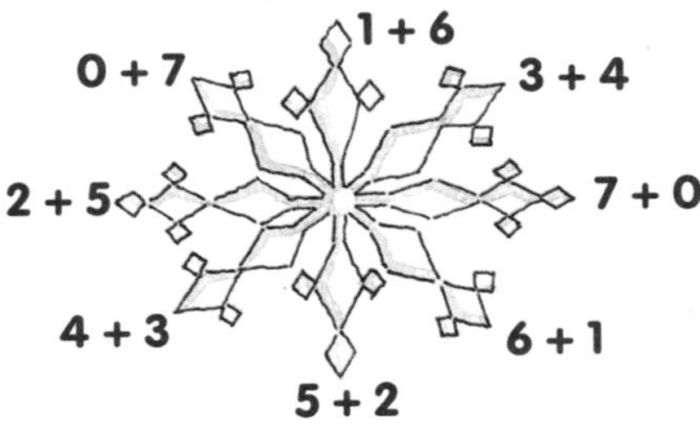

There are five bees outside the beehive.

Along come three more bees.

Now there are eight bees outside the beehive.

five bees + three bees = eight bees $5 + 3 = 8$

Here are six flags.

Here are two more flags.

There are eight flags altogether.

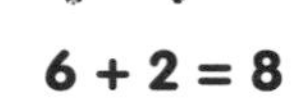

six flags + two flags = eight flags $6 + 2 = 8$

REMEMBER $5 + 3 = 8$ $6 + 2 = 8$

There are eight sailing boats in the race.
Each boat should have a number on its sail,
but two boats have their numbers missing.

What are the missing numbers?

Try to learn all the number bonds that make up eight.
They are shown on the sails of the yachts.

Here are five bottles.

Here are another four bottles.

There are nine bottles altogether.

five bottles + four bottles = nine bottles $5 + 4 = 9$

Tessa has three sweets.

Tommy has six sweets.

Altogether, they have nine sweets.

three sweets + six sweets = nine sweets $3 + 6 = 9$

REMEMBER $5 + 4 = 9$ $3 + 6 = 9$

Can you do these sums?

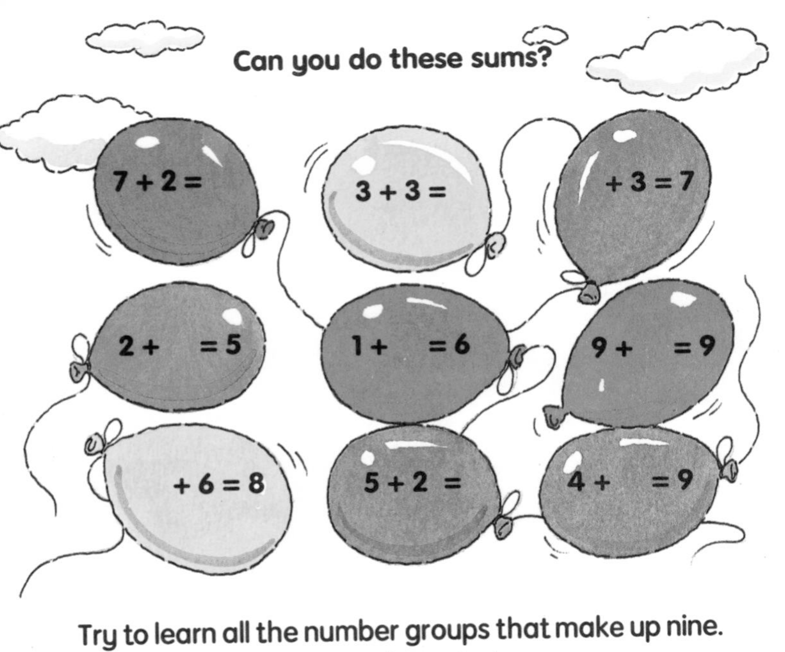

Try to learn all the number groups that make up nine.
They are shown below.

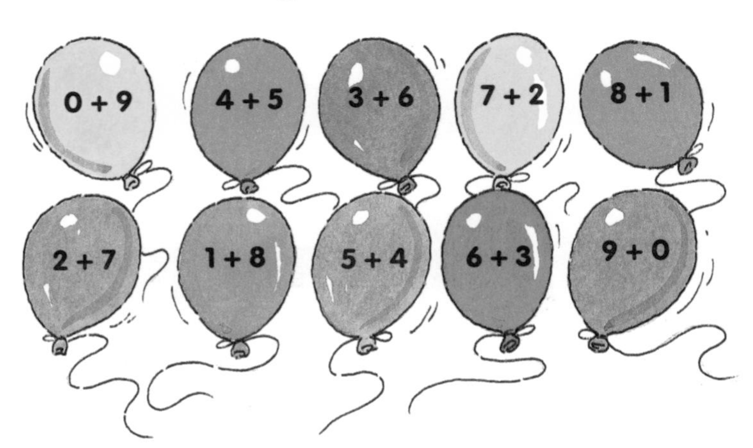

Up the ladders and down the snakes

These sums go up the ladders, from **1** to **9**, and down the snakes, from **9** to **1**. Can you fill in the missing numbers in each sum?

5 + = 9
5 + = 8
4 + = 7
3 + = 6
2 + = 5
1 + = 4
1 + = 3
0 + = 2
1 + = 1

3 + = 9
4 + = 8
6 + = 7
0 + = 6
3 + = 5
2 + = 4
2 + = 3
1 + = 2
0 + = 1

 + 7 = 9
 + 5 = 8
 + 1 = 7
 + 2 = 6
 + 1 = 5
 + 4 = 4
 + 3 = 3
 + 1 = 2
 + 0 = 1

4 + 5 =
2 + 6 =
3 + 4 =
1 + 5 =
5 + 0 =
3 + 1 =
3 + 0 =
1 + 1 =
1 + 0 =

Collecting balls

Match the groups to the correct monkey.

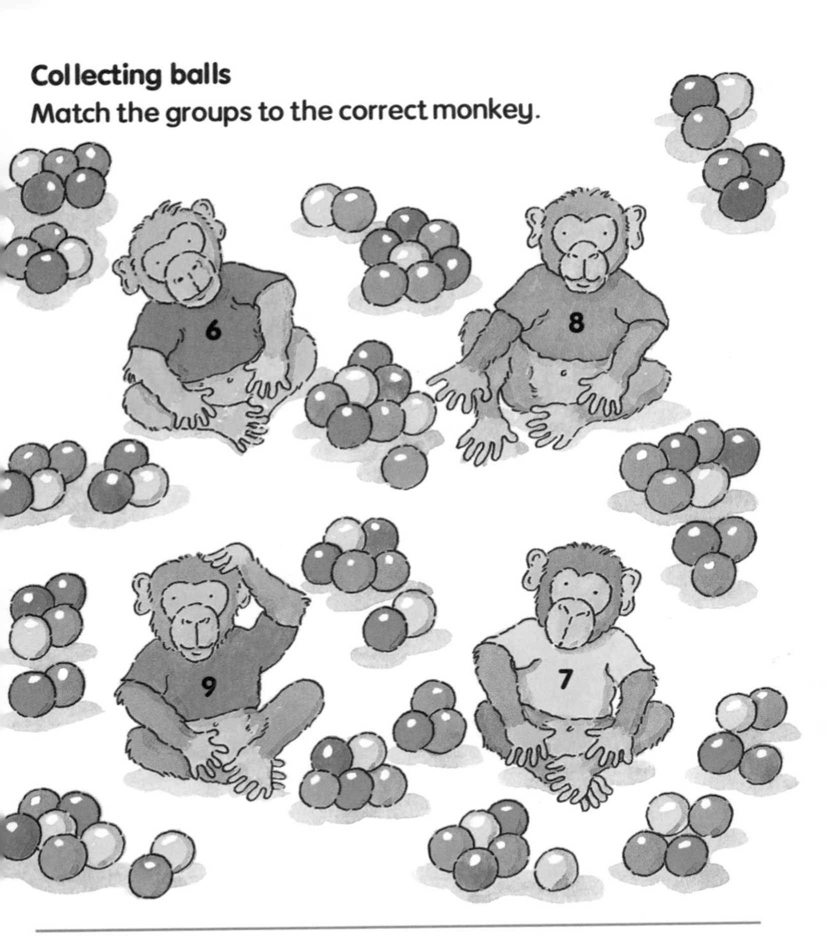

Count in 2s

2 – 4 –	3 – 5 –	5 – 7 –
1 – – 5	– 4 – 6	– 7 – 9

Tessa has four coins.

Tommy has six coins.

Altogether, they have ten coins.

four coins + six coins = ten coins

$4 + 6 = 10$

Tessa has seven coins.

Tommy has three coins.

They have ten coins in all.

seven coins + three coins = ten coins

$7 + 3 = 10$

REMEMBER | $4 + 6 = 10$ | $7 + 3 = 10$

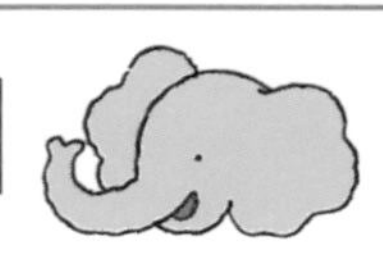

Is there enough in the purse?

You need ten coins to buy a strawberry ice-cream, nine coins to buy a chocolate one, eight coins for a peppermint one, and seven coins for a vanilla ice-cream. Can you decide which ice-cream you can afford with the coins in each purse?

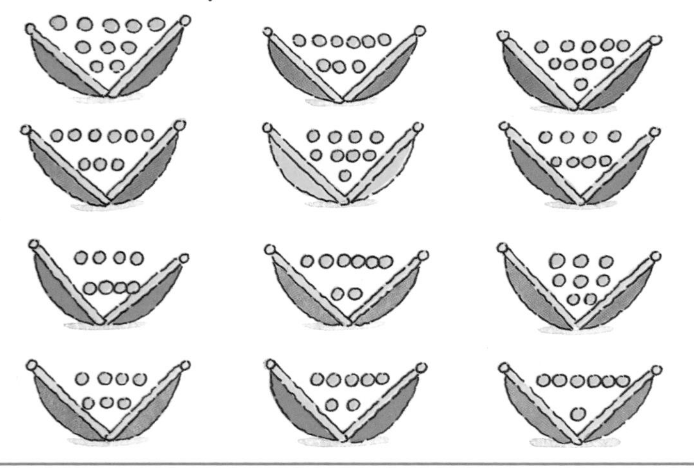

Try to learn all the number groups that make up ten. They are shown below.

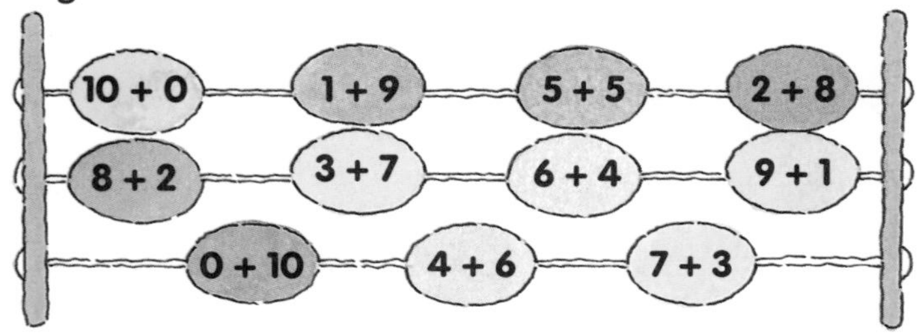

This witch has seven broomsticks.

This witch has four broomsticks.

Altogether, the witches have eleven broomsticks.

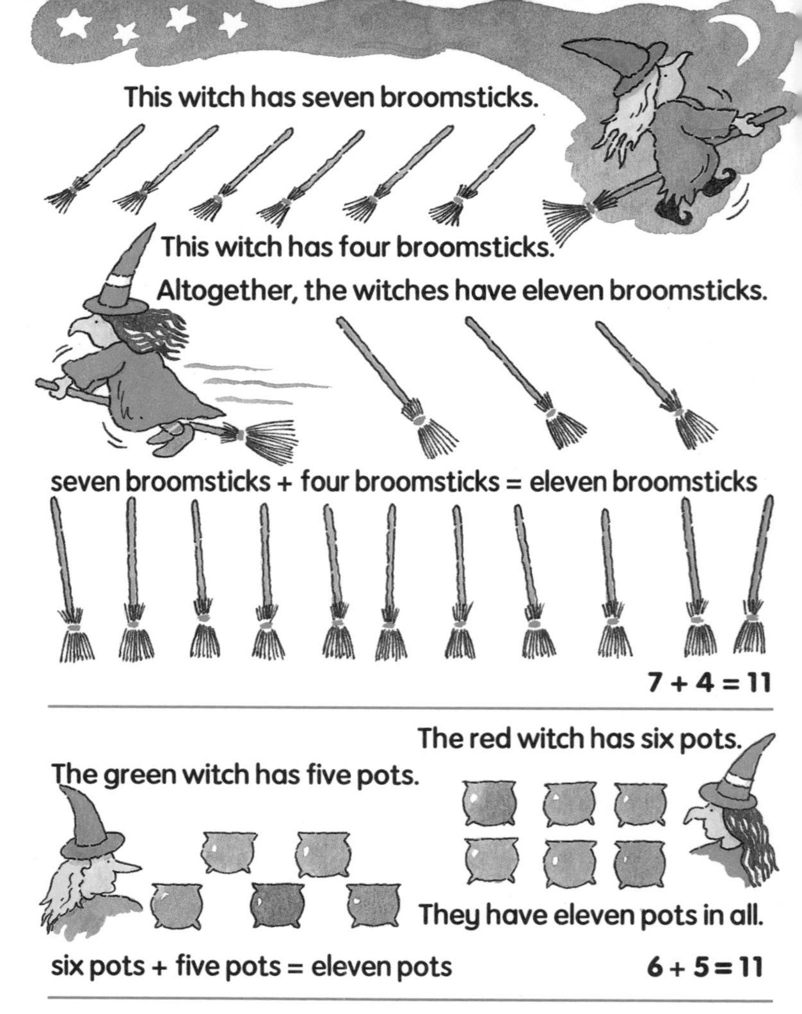

seven broomsticks + four broomsticks = eleven broomsticks

$7 + 4 = 11$

The red witch has six pots.

The green witch has five pots.

They have eleven pots in all.

six pots + five pots = eleven pots

$6 + 5 = 11$

REMEMBER | $7 + 4 = 11$ | $6 + 5 = 11$

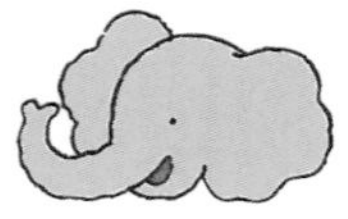

Tadpole totals

There are lots of tadpoles in these bowls. Can you work out how many there are in each bowl? How many bowls contain eleven tadpoles?

Count in 3s

3 – 6 –	1 – 4 –	5 – 8 –
4 – – 10	2 – – 8	– 6 – 9

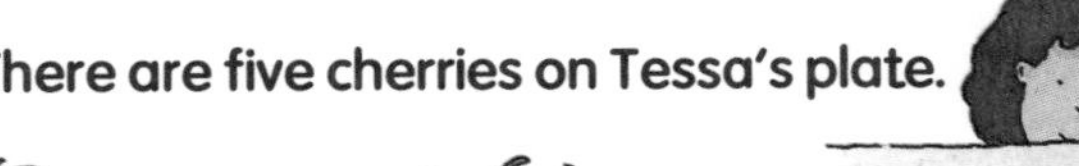

There are five cherries on Tessa's plate.

There are seven cherries on Tommy's plate.

Altogether, they have twelve cherries.

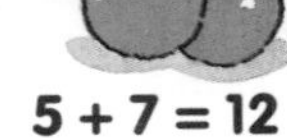

five cherries + seven cherries = twelve cherries

5 + 7 = 12

There are eight cherries on this cake.

There are four cherries on this cake.

There are twelve cherries in all.

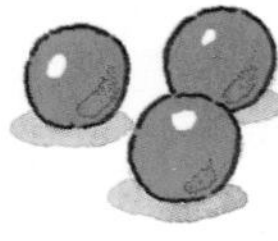

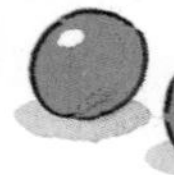

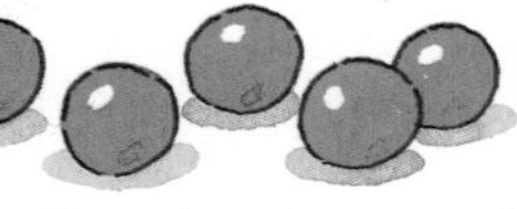

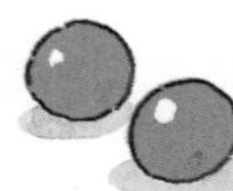

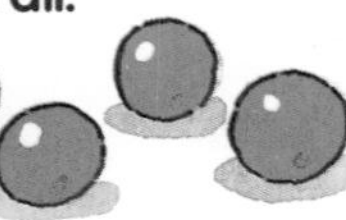

eight cherries + four cherries = twelve cherries

8 + 4 = 12

REMEMBER | **5 + 7 = 12** | **8 + 4 = 12**

Can you do these sums?

8 + 4 =

5 + 5 =

+ 7 = 10

4 + = 11

7 + = 12

6 + = 10

2 + 10 =

+ 6 = 11

3 + 8 =

8 + 2 =

2 + 9 =

+ 6 = 12

Count in 4s

1 – 5 –	4 – – 12	
0 – – 8	2 – 6 –	– 7 – 11

Magic Square

All the lines of numbers in this square, across, down, or diagonally, add up to 12. Can you fill in the missing numbers? The answer is printed upside-down at the foot of the page.

3	4	
		2
3	4	

The route to 12

Start at A and take whichever route gets to the answer at B

A: Start   B: Finish

2 + 3 +   1 + 1

1 + 1 + 2 + 4 + 2 + 3 = 12

3 + 1 +   4 + 2

Odd numbers

Put a ring round each of the odd numbers in this list.

12 7 5 6 8 11 9 3 2 4

Even numbers

Put a ring round each of the even numbers in this list.

9 8 7 4 1 2 10 11 6 12

3	4	5
6	4	2
3	4	5

A number maze

Can you find the right way through this number maze? Starting at the top, move from box to box, sideways, downwards, or diagonally. You can only move onto boxes where the sum adds up to 12.

	?	?	?	
11 + 2	8 + 4	3 + 9	2 + 10	6 + 7
6 + 6	6 + 5	6 + 2	2 + 9	4 + 6
3 + 7	7 + 5	9 + 3	8 + 4	8 + 5
1 + 12	7 + 3	2 + 9	9 + 3	2 + 11
7 + 6	2 + 8	5 + 7	7 + 7	8 + 6
8 + 10	1 + 9	8 + 3	3 + 9	9 + 4
6 + 5	6 + 5	10 + 4	2 + 10	2 + 8
7 + 4	6 + 6	4 + 8	7 + 4	3 + 8
			12 + 0	= 12

Count to twelve

	1	2	3	4	5	6	7	8	9	10	11	12
in 2s:	1	2	3	4	5	6	7	8	9	10	11	12
in 3s:	1	2	3	4	5	6	7	8	9	10	11	12
in 4s:	1	2	3	4	5	6	7	8	9	10	11	12
in 6s:	1	2	3	4	5	6	7	8	9	10	11	12

0 + 0 = 0

0 + 1 = 1   1 + 0 = 1

0 + 2 = 2   2 + 0 = 2   1 + 1 = 2

0 + 3 = 3   3 + 0 = 3   1 + 2 = 3   2 + 1 = 3

0 + 4 = 4   4 + 0 = 4   1 + 3 = 4   3 + 1 = 4   2 + 2 = 4

0 + 5 = 5   5 + 0 = 5   1 + 4 = 5   4 + 1 = 5   2 + 3 = 5   3 + 2 = 5

0 + 6 = 6   6 + 0 = 6   1 + 5 = 6   5 + 1 = 6   2 + 4 = 6   4 + 2 = 6

0 + 7 = 7   7 + 0 = 7   1 + 6 = 7   6 + 1 = 7   2 + 5 = 7   5 + 2 = 7

0 + 8 = 8   8 + 0 = 8   1 + 7 = 8   7 + 1 = 8   2 + 6 = 8   6 + 2 = 8

0 + 9 = 9   9 + 0 = 9   1 + 8 = 9   8 + 1 = 9   2 + 7 = 9   7 + 2 = 9

0 + 10 = 10   10 + 0 = 10   1 + 9 = 10   9 + 1 = 10   2 + 8 = 10   8 + 2 = 10

0 + 11 = 11   11 + 0 = 11   1 + 10 = 11   10 + 1 = 11   2 + 9 = 11   9 + 2 = 11

0 + 12 = 12   12 + 0 = 12   1 + 11 = 12   11 + 1 = 12   2 + 10 = 12   10 + 2 = 12

ODD NUMBERS AND EVEN NUMBERS

1 2 **3** 4 **5** 6 **7** 8 **9** 10 **11** 12 **13** 14 **15** 16 **17** 18 **19** 20

All the numbers in **heavy type** are called the 'odd numbers'.

1 **2** 3 **4** 5 **6** 7 **8** 9 **10** 11 **12** 13 **14** 15 **16** 17 **18** 19 **20**

All the numbers in **heavy type** are called the 'even numbers'.

DIGITS

The individual numerals we use for all maths work are called 'digits'. These digits are **0, 1, 2, 3, 4, 5, 6, 7, 8, 9.**

TENS AND UNITS

Numbers from **10** to **99** are shown as 'tens' and 'units'. The first digit shows how many 'tens' there are in the number. The second digit shows how many 'units' there are. The number **13** is made up of **1** 'ten' and **3** 'units'. Number **79** is made up of **7** 'tens' and **9** 'units'.